Part Order Colour Code

 Cross Point

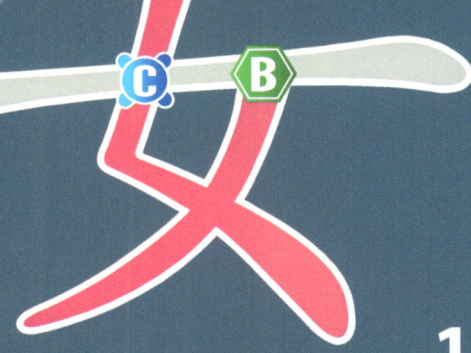
Bond Point

Dot Last

Dot

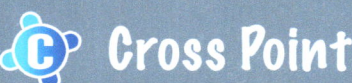
Cross Point

2

肉丸
ròu wán

meatballs

RL-Slash

RL-Slash Intersects

蜂蜜
fēng mì

honey

3

猪
zhū

pig

RL-Slash

RL-Slash Intersects

身体
shēn tǐ

body

5

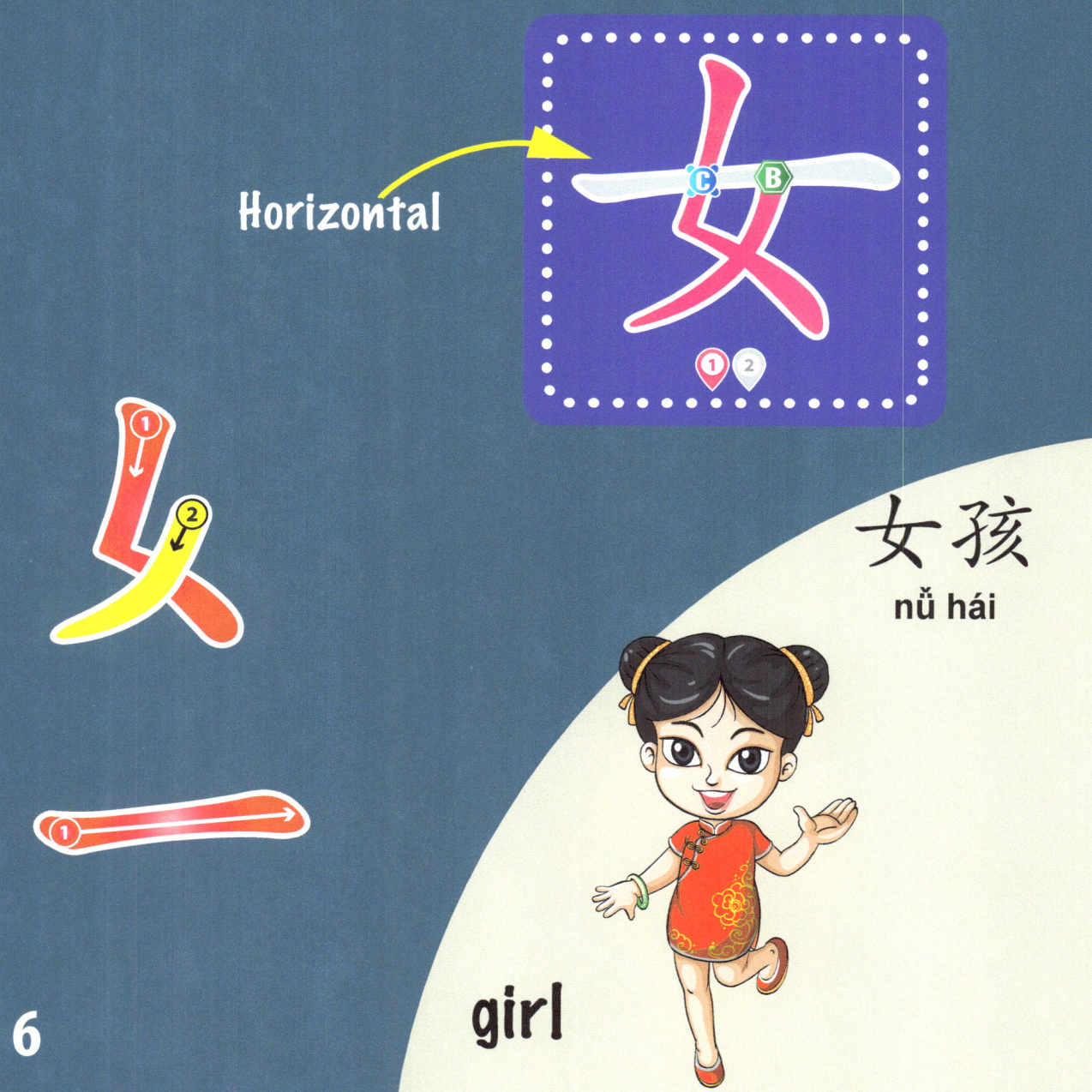

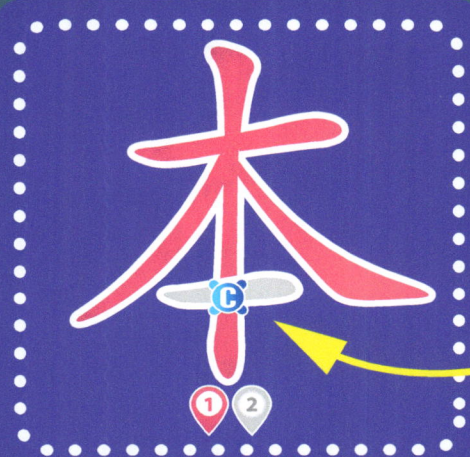

Horizontal Last

Horizontal

本子
běn zi

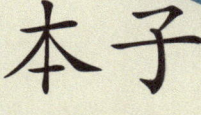

notebook

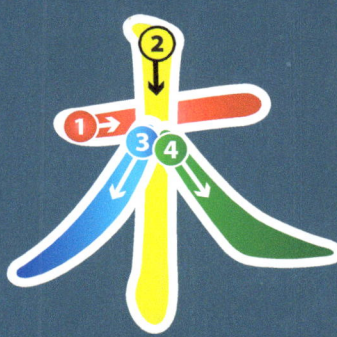

Horizontal

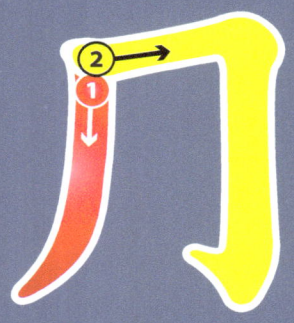

栅栏
zhà lán

fence

Horizontal

Horizontal Last

牡丹
mǔ dān

peony

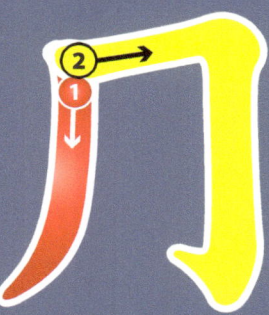

Horizontal

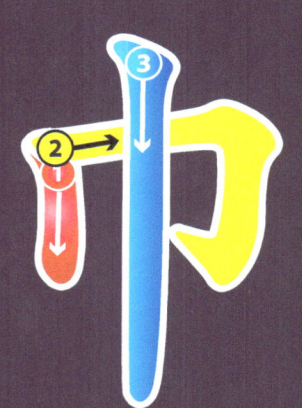

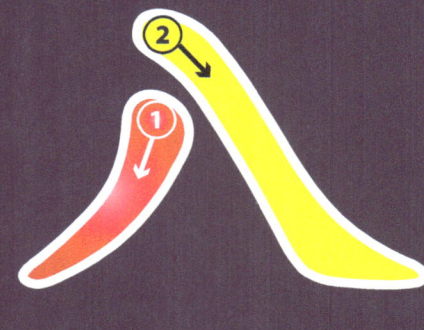

10

刺
ci

thorn

Horizontal

Intersects Horizontal

花束
huā shù

bouquet

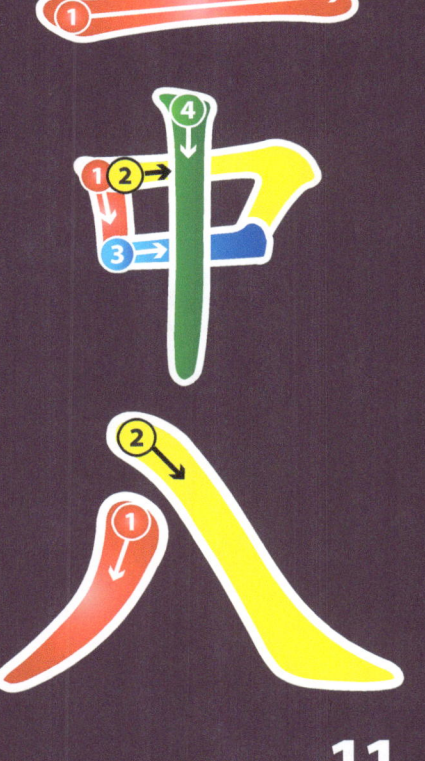

11

Horizontal

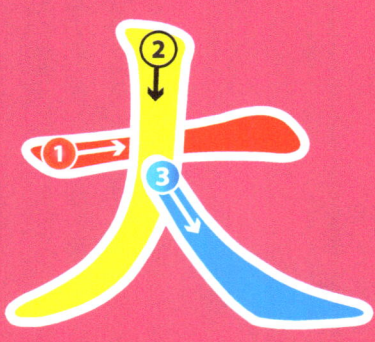

衣夹
yī jiā

clothes peg

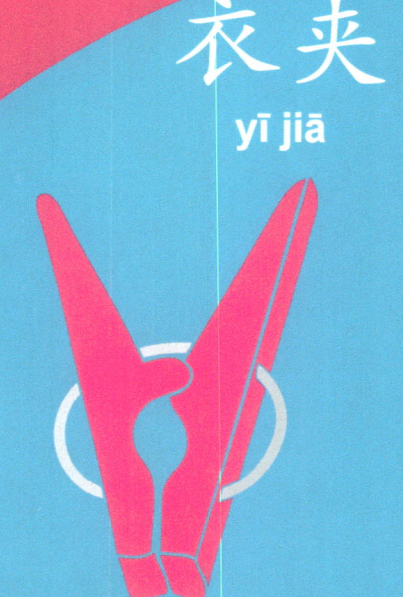

Intersects Horizontal

Horizontal

练习
liàn xí
practice

13

Horizontals

砖块
zhuān kuài

brick

Intersects 2 Horizontals

Horizontals

钱
qián

money

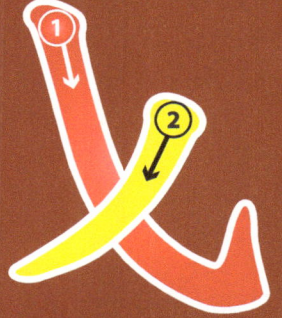

15

 C-Frame

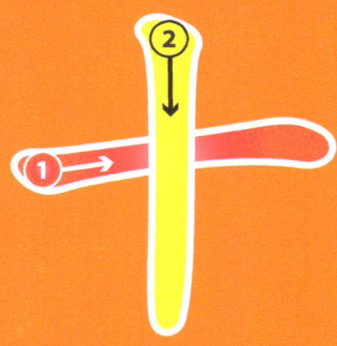

车子
chē zi

car

Intersects C-Frame

C-Frame

牙
yá

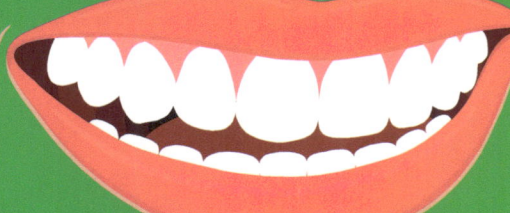
teeth

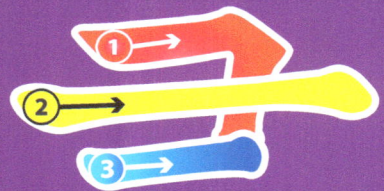 **Flipped-C**

芦笋
lú sǔn

asparagus

Intersects
Flipped-C

Flipped-C

狒狒
fèi fèi

baboon

 Enclosure

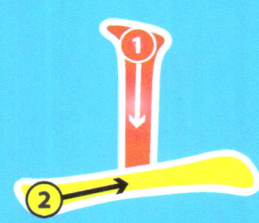

虫子
chóng zi

worm

Intersects
Enclosure

晚上
wăn shang

Enclosure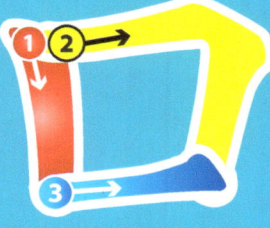

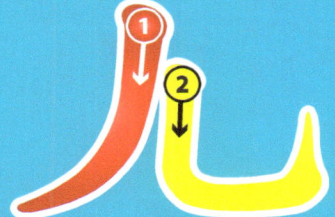

night

21

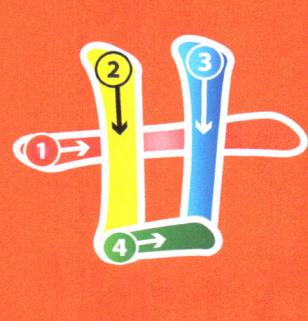

 Enclosure

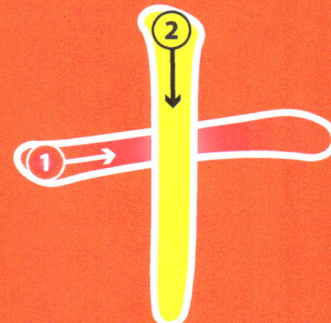

鞋子
xié zi

shoes

伸展
shēn zhǎn
stretching

**Intersects
Enclosure**

Enclosure

 Enclosure

里面
lǐ miàn

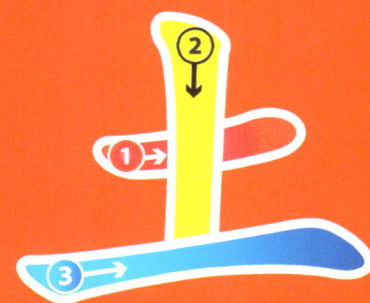

inside

Intersects Enclosure

水果
shuǐ guǒ

fruits

Enclosure

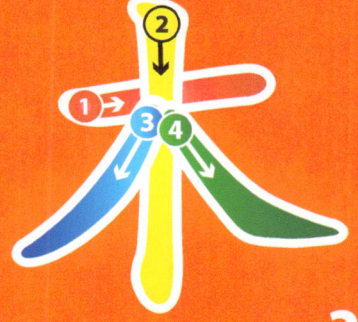

25

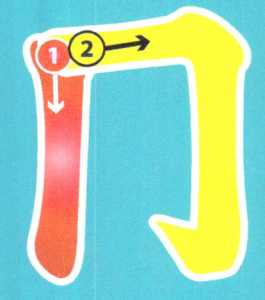 n-Frame

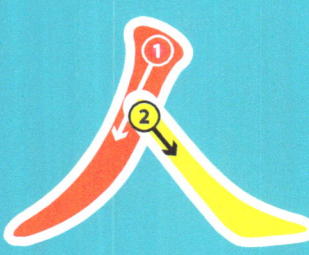

ròu

meat

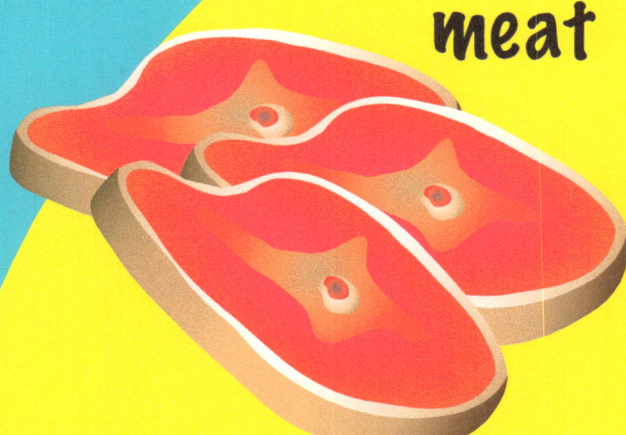

Intersects
n-Frame

两个
liǎng gè

two

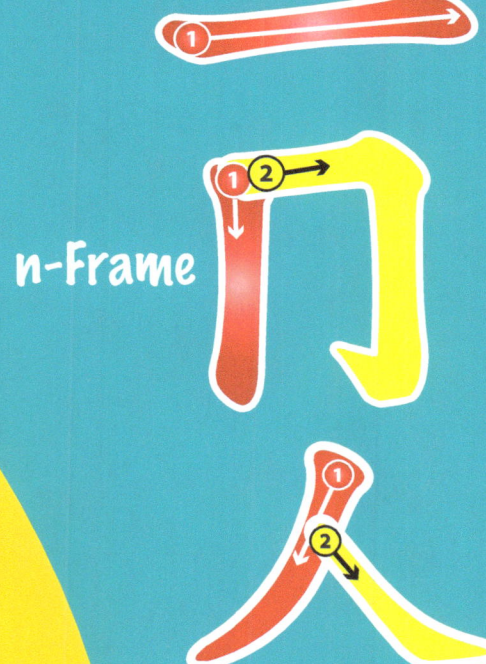

n-Frame

 n-Frame

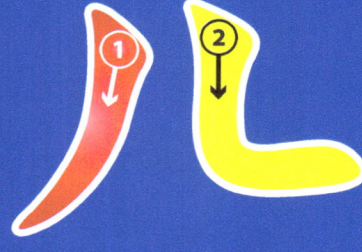

西瓜
xī guā

water-melon

Intersects
n-Frame

再见
zài jiàn

goodbye

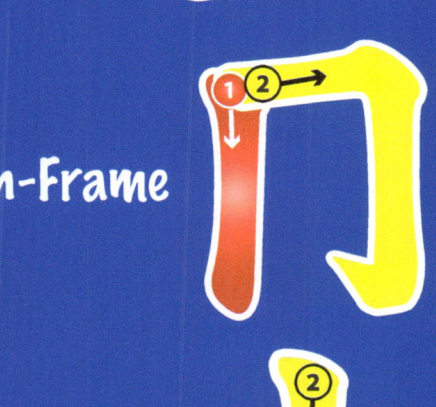

n-Frame

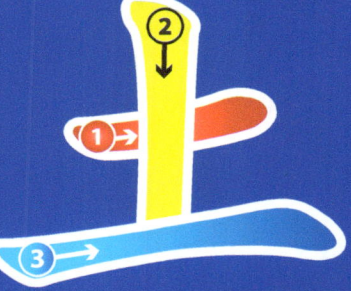

一 刀 十 丶

n-Frame

30

甫
① ② ③ ④ ⑤ ⑥

捕鱼
bǔ yú

fishing

Intersects U-Frame

逆风
nì fēng

go against the wind

U-Frame

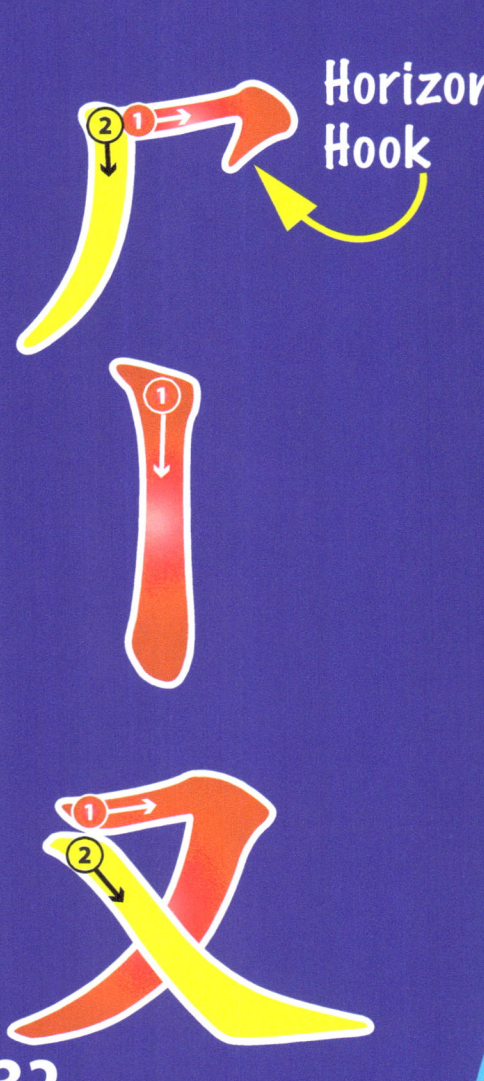
Horizontal Hook

皮夹
pí jiā

leather wallet

Intersects Horizontal Hook

Horizontal Hook

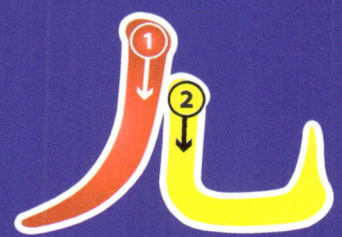

枕头
zhěn tou

pillow